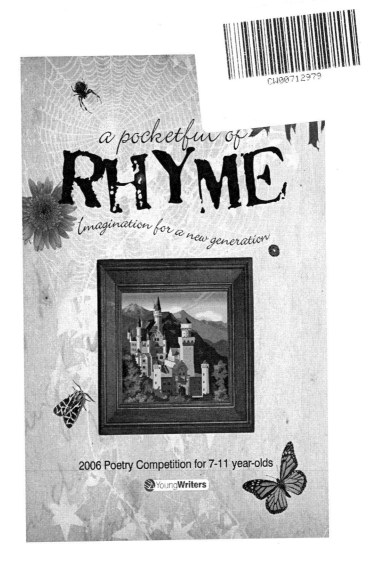

a pocketful of

RHYME

Imagination for a new generation

2006 Poetry Competition for 7-11 year-olds

YoungWriters

The East Midlands Vol II
Edited by Heather Killingray

 Young**Writers**

First published in Great Britain in 2006 by:
Young Writers
Remus House
Coltsfoot Drive
Peterborough
PE2 9JX
Telephone: 01733 890066
Website: www.youngwriters.co.uk

SB ISBN 1 84602 568 0

Foreword

Young Writers was established in 1991 and has been passionately devoted to the promotion of reading and writing in children and young adults ever since. The quest continues today. Young Writers remains as committed to the nurturing of poetic and literary talent as ever.

This year's Young Writers competition has proven as vibrant and dynamic as ever and we are delighted to present a showcase of the best poetry from across the UK and in some cases overseas. Each poem has been selected from a wealth of *A Pocketful Of Rhyme* entries before ultimately being published in this, our fourteenth primary school poetry series.

Once again, we have been supremely impressed by the overall quality of the entries we have received. The imagination, energy and creativity which has gone into each young writer's entry made choosing the poems a challenging and often difficult but ultimately hugely rewarding task - the general high standard of the work submitted ensured this opportunity to bring their poetry to a larger appreciative audience.

We sincerely hope you are pleased with this final collection and that you will enjoy *A Pocketful Of Rhyme The East Midlands Vol II* for many years to come.

Contents

James Burrows (9)   79
Ruth Page (8)   80
Edward Hirst (9)   81
Adam Russell (9)   82
Bharath Sharma (9)   83

St Werburgh's CE Primary School, Derby

Joanna Wallace (11)   84
Lauren Collings (11)   85
Kirsty Fazekas (11)   86
Ben Knapp (10)   87
Katie Pealing (10)   88
Alex Revill (11)   89
Kirsten Fooks (10)   90
Grace Gillam (10)   91
Joe Wreford (10)   92
Tess Clark (10)   93
Thomas Fearn-Wright (11)   94
Liam Slaney (11)   95
Joe Wood (11)   96
Sam Wreford (10)   97
Ben Taylor (11)   98
Amy Harvey (10)   99
Abigail Anderson (10)   100
Bronte Owen (10)   101
Katie Roethenbaugh (10)   102
Joshua Large (10)   103
Bethany Marshall (10)   104
Amy Stephenson (8)   105
Danielle Harvey (8)   106
Ellie Hill (9)   107
Idony Baker-Hodkinson (8)   108
Jordan Cook (11)   109
Dylan Mahowa (11)   110
Kyle Weeks (9)   111
Joshua Cook (11)   112
Ryan Fayers (10)   113
Jamie Baker (11)   114
Benjamin Wilford (11)   115
Corey Moore (8)   116
Kieran Truby-Ware (10)   117

Richard Allen (11)   118
Liam Marshall (8)   119
Katy Birch (8)   120
Ellie Beech (8)   121
Ethan Beardsley (8)   122
Becky Reeves (8)   123
Alex Nicholls (8)   124
Ella O'Neill (8)   125
Chloe Oxley (7)   126
Jake Stoddart (8)   127
Saul Shields (10)   128
Laura Milner (8)   129
Natasha Marshall (8)   130

Silverstone CE Junior School, Towcester

Dan French (9)   131
Philippa Sutton (11)   132
Evie Dibble (10)   133
Jack Shaw (10)   134
Megan Goodman (10)   135
Toby Dennison (9)   136
Chloe Challinger (10)   137
Hannah Sylvester (10)   138
Campbell Taylor (10)   139
Jordan Knight (10)   140
Nathan Rogers (10)   141
Isabel Garriock (10)   142
Calum Kerns (10)   143
Edward Measey (10)   144
Christina Cooper (11)   145
Tiana Djahanbakhsh (11)   146
Oliver Hinton (11)   147
Zuzanna Paveley (11)   148
Joe Read (11)   149
Aaron Culley (11)   150
Emilie Sylvester (11)   151
Anna Lawson (11)   152
Francesca Hudson (8)   153
Adam Dearsley (7)   154
Benjamin Webb (11)   155
Marcus Culley (11)   156

George Goodman (7)   157
Nicole Djahanbakhsh (8)   158
Maxwell Cawthorne (7)   159
Hannah Pace (8)   160
Jake Van Kampen (9)   161
Christopher Hinton (8)   162
Thomas Elmstrom (7)   163
Jack Haywood (8)   164
Emma Measey (8)   165
Madeleine Smee (9)   166
Shannon Webb (9)   167
Christian Loveless (9)   168
Louis McKendry (9)   169
Zoe Stockley (9)   170
Charlotte Lloyd (9)   171
Conor Young (9)   172
Jack Hales (9)   173
Robyn Edwards (8)   174
Emily Libich (9)   175
Jonathan Howse (9)   176
Luke Heavey (10)   177

Swaffham Prior CE Primary School, Swaffham Prior

Leanne Wilson (9)   178
Charlotte Elston (9)   179
Richard Terrington (8)   180
Hannah Eaton (9)   181
Emilia Hubbard (7)   182
Harry Doe (9)   183
Adam Tarasewicz (8)   184
Henry Kingsmill (9)   185
Emma Hodge (8)   186
Kasia Tabecka (8)   187
Rosie Robinson (8)   188
Maddie Lewinski (8)   189
Jessica Hill (8)   190
Cleo McGregor (8)   191
Ayshea Blanks (8)   192
Becky Arksey (8)   193
Mia Blanks (8)   194
Helena Pumfrey (8)   195

The Poems

King Kong

Ground smasher
Plane crasher
Car flipper
Flesh ripper
Bamboo chomper
People stomper
Jaw breaker
Log thrower
Civilization terroriser
Building climber
Roarer!

Will Stephens (9)
Ely St John's Primary School, Ely

Rose

The scent of new life
The face of an angel
A skin of deep red
As light as a feather
Too much for the weather
It's thinner than leather
But thicker than a feather.

Misha Van Wright Mellage (8)
Ely St John's Primary School, Ely

As, As, As . . .

As pretty as a flower
As tall as a tower
As shiny as a star
As big as a bar
As nice as love
As gentle as a dove
As smelly as feet
As comfy as a seat
As high as the sky
As tasty as pie
As good as a book
As good as you look
As fast as a car
As clear as a jar
As cute as a girl
As precious as a pearl
As hot as a fire
As sparkly as sapphire
As, as, as!

Ariana Smyth-Schaal (9)
Ely St John's Primary School, Ely

King Kong

Man eater
Bone crusher
Skull ripper
Limb tearer
Heart squasher
Brain pulper
Soul destroyer
Car breaker
Island controller
Hairy horror
Monkey maniac
Ape monster
Organ muncher
Breath extinguisher
Primate terror lord

It's not ethical!

Jacob Pake (9)
Ely St John's Primary School, Ely

As, As, As . . .

As large as a whale
As small as a snail
As tall as a giraffe
As funny as a laugh
As big as King Kong
As loud as ding-dong
As mean as my sister
As hurtful as a blister
As weird as my brother
As warm as my cover
As slimy as a slug
As black as a bug.

Sarah Lappin (9)
Ely St John's Primary School, Ely

Poppy

P oppy's cute and cuddly

O bviously she's lovely, sometimes bad and naughty but we still

love her

P urring all day and all night

P aws are on cats, they lick them when they are dirty

Y ou would love my Poppy as much as I do.

Mia Turner (8)
Ely St John's Primary School, Ely

As, As, As . . .

As slow as a snail
As big as a whale
As small as a mouse
As big as a house
As strong as King Kong
As loud as ding-dong
As buzzy as a bee
As small as can be
As green as grass
As shiny as brass
As fat as a fist
As long as a list
As ugly as a pig
As yucky as a fig
As annoying as my brother
As lovely as my mother
As slippery as a snake
As juicy as a steak
As pretty as me
As far as you can see
As cosy as my bed
As heavy as lead
As yummy as ice cream
As sweet as a dream
As noisy as a drill
As good as The Bill
As fat as a cow
As quiet as a miaow
As lazy as a cat
As quick as a bat
As fast as a cheetah
As hot as a heater.

Zoe Symonds (9)
Ely St John's Primary School, Ely

In My History Lesson

Romans, Saxons, Celts
Soldiers in big belts
Wars, enemies, battles
Lots of sheep, rabbits and cattle.

Forts, castles, hills
Slavery, sweeping cotton mills
Towers, bridges and Hadrian's Wall
Not many games and no shopping malls.

Tori Gibbons (9)
Ely St John's Primary School, Ely

As, As, As . . .

As light as a feather
As bad as the weather
As soft as a pillow
As small as a bee
As silly as me
As big as a boat
As deep as a moat
As fluffy as sheep
As long as sleep
As bored as a sigh
As sad as a cry
As tired as a yawn
As bright as the dawn
As soft as down
As long as a gown.

Megan Coulson (9)
Ely St John's Primary School, Ely

My Cousin Charlie

My cousin is special in different ways
He may not understand
He might throw his beaker in the river or run away.

My cousin is special in different ways
He always runs up to you and hugs you
And loves his trampoline
And is obsessed with Postman Pat and Jess.

My cousin is special in different ways
The only sad thing about it is we worry about his future
But he soon takes our minds off it by making us laugh
And making us feel warm inside.

My cousin is special in different ways
He is special
My cousin Charlie is autistic.

Even though he's autistic I love him still
And I hope he loves me the same way.

Molly Butler (8)
Ely St John's Primary School, Ely

Animals

I like rabbits
They like carrots
I like fish
They like a dish
I like cats
They like rats
I like dogs
They like bogs
I like pigs
They like figs
I like crocs
They like rocks.

Tom Walker (9)
Ely St John's Primary School, Ely

Dalmatian Poem

It's black and white with spots or splodges and very tame too
If you ever got one it would certainly look after you.
It is black and white or maybe brown and white.
It likes long walks and likes to run, and it enjoys lots and lots of fun.
It goes *woof, woof* as it wags its tail.
If it entered a dog show it would certainly not fail.
Dalmatians are lovely.

Indi-Fern Trainer (8)
Ely St John's Primary School, Ely

As, As, As . . .

As boring as school
As big as a hall
As small as a mouse
As tall as a house
As quick as a flash
As fast as a dash
As kind as a mum
As sweet as a hum
As fun as a ride
As posh as a bride.

Jessica Courdelle (9)
Ely St John's Primary School, Ely

The Legend Of Romulus And Remus

There's a famous story of how Rome got its name
Some boys called Romulus and Remus
At the emperor's house he said, 'You must make a city,' and that's
what they did.
They did not know what to call it,
Emperor put a line in the sky and that's why it's called Rome.

Dalton Orchard (9)
Ely St John's Primary School, Ely

As, As, As . . .

As fast as a plane
As soft as a mane
As quick as a flick
As sick as a tick
As strong as a bat
As gentle as a cat
As large as a whale
As tall as a male
As pretty as a flower
As firm as a tower
As nasty as a bear
As ugly as a pear.

Conor Logan (9)
Ely St John's Primary School, Ely

Smelly Woods

Little bud, sloppy mud
Tree branches, dirty dancers
Dirty phones, non-battery phones
Ghost trees, stinging bees
Football shoe, empty loo
High wood, big flood
Pitch-black, broken father's back
Slithering snake, bake a cake
Colourful parrots, look like carrots
Slithering fish in a dish.

Lewis Banks (9)
Fernwood Junior School, Nottingham

I Have Got . . .

Ten Dalmatians, all spotty and lively
Nine Yorkshire terriers, tiny and yappy
Eight Labradors, curly tails sticking out
Seven bloodhounds, all wrinkled and grumpy
Six sausage dogs, all long and slow
Five poodles, pink, purple and white
Four foxhounds, ready to hunt
Three Border terriers, chasing after me
Two greyhounds, all skinny and bony
One . . . me.

Chloe Plant (9)
Fernwood Junior School, Nottingham

Giraffe

G ay and joyful giraffes are
I n the zoo where animals are kept
R oyal giraffes are in the sky
A nd they are taller than a mansion
F alling from the sky, they land on soft clouds
F is for friends who play with me
E lephants are stomping as loud as can be and I'm trying to go
to sleep!

Azeem Mahmood (9)
Fernwood Junior School, Nottingham

Amy's Pets

Amy has . . .
Ten tarantulas that crawl on your face
Nine nasty gnats that bite you in the night
Eight enormous elephants that shake the ground
Seven snakes slithering on my floor
Six snails that make lots of trails
Five fish in a bowl
Four flamingos standing on one leg
Three tigers stalking for prey
Two tooth fairies who give you money
One . . . guess what? Me!

Amy Williams (9)
Fernwood Junior School, Nottingham

Name Alphabet

A is for Amy who likes to run around
B is for Ben who lies on the ground
C is for Carl who loves his toys
D is for David who hates all the boys
E is for Emma who plays all the time
F is for Fiasal who eats lots of lime
G is for George who likes to eat cake
H is for Henry who drinks from the lake
I is for Isaac who's learning to spell
J is for James who has a bad smell
K is for Katie who eats a lot
L is for Lewis who has a big spot
M is for Matthew who is very old
N is for Nicky who is very cold
O is for Oliver who likes to eat
P is for Peter who doesn't eat meat.

Amun Johal (9)
Fernwood Junior School, Nottingham

Holidays

H ot, warm days in the summer, my face is

O h so red, and the breeze is nowhere to be found

L ollies are melting in the sparkling sun

I cky, muggy hands are touching the sea

D ad and Mum keep throwing me in the sea

A jellyfish will come to the shore

Y our mum will get stung

S o go to the beach and have some fun!

Katie Daley (9)
Fernwood Junior School, Nottingham

Animals A-D

A is for animals who are grazing in the daylight
B is for bats who fly through the night
C is for cats prowling through the night, they have very good eyesight
D is for dogs all furry and bright.

Aleshanee Nagi (8)
Fernwood Junior School, Nottingham

Doctor Who

D octor Who is always there
O h there are so many monsters
C ybermen shout, 'Delete, delete!'
T he Tardis is so wicked and so fast
'O h exterminate,' cried the Daleks
R ose is a great helper

W here are we?
H ere we are
O h, we are in a spaceship.

James Goodall (9)
Fernwood Junior School, Nottingham

Pong Wiffy

P owerful stenches come from the wood
O h what a smell it makes
N obody dares go into the woods
G reat brambles grow in there

W itches live in there people say
I stay inside when it smells
F ish stink like rotten eggs
F ood tastes like nothing
Y et I wonder, why is this?

Ben Butler (9)
Fernwood Junior School, Nottingham

A, B, C,

A is for the world's animals
   who light up in the dark night.
B is for the flying black bats
   who sleep through the day light.
C is for the gentle moving cats
   who cuddle others and purr.
D is for rough playing dogs
   who scratch away their fur.

Charlie Brice (9)
Fernwood Junior School, Nottingham

Nature

Nature is so bright
It fills my veins with light.
Look at all the things around
Confused, my thoughts go round.
Big, tall trees
Arranged in threes.
Lots of leaves
A chilling breeze.
Lots of logs
Three stray dogs.
Lots of rubbish
A book published.
Look at all the broken glass
Sometimes covered in grass.

Alex Marner (8)
Fernwood Junior School, Nottingham

Animals

A is for animals that lie in the scorching sun
B is for bats that fly in the blackboard sky for fun
C is for travelling camels that travel through the burning sand
D is for Dalmatian dogs that dance throughout the land
E is for elephants that stomp loudly through a farm
F is for frogs that hop inside a barn.

Sarah Allen (9)
Fernwood Junior School, Nottingham

Sophie's Pets

S mall and fluffy rabbits hopping round
O ur rooms are full of pets
P ets are cute and fluffy
H ouses are full of pets bouncing round all day
I cky spiders crawling on the ground
E lephants banging on the floor, messing everything up
S nakes slithering across the floor

P eople love pets just like they do
E ating and sleeping all they do
T igers roaring all around
S piders crawling across the floor.

Sophie Barnes (9)
Fernwood Junior School, Nottingham

Georgia's Pets

Georgia has . . .
Ten fat dogs who chew Dad's slippers
Nine mean cats who chase rats
Eight fish who swim all day non-stop
Seven rabbits that never stop chewing carrots
Six horses that gallop all night
Five guinea pigs that never stop trying to escape
Four snakes that never stop slithering
Three turtles that take a month to get upstairs
Two huge hippos that wreck the house
One elephant that ruins my new flowers.

Georgia Eady (9)
Fernwood Junior School, Nottingham

A, B, C, D

A is for apple
   that can be green.
B is for bed
   where I go to sleep.
C is for cow
   that eats the grass.
D is for dig
   that I do in the sand.

Mia Noble (9)
Fernwood Junior School, Nottingham

Food

Soggy sausages in spicy sauce
A massive meatball, munch, munch
Ugly potatoes covered in beans
Smelly sardines, what's for lunch?
Apple pudding, yum, yum, yum
Gorgeous gum, strawberry taste
Extra, extra juicy plum
Slippy, slurpy spaghetti.

Ruby Guyler (9)
Fernwood Junior School, Nottingham

My Sister

My sister is very tall
She's nearly seventeen
Her face is all mouldy
She thinks she is the queen.

Her nose is just so pointy
It looks like a big nail
Every maths test she takes
She's guaranteed to fail.

Her favourite animal is a lion
Oh well, what can they do?
They're not going to bite her
Especially in a zoo.

My sister is a black belt
But I can beat her up
She says it's very easy
So I just trip her up.

Liam Gregory (10)
Fernwood Junior School, Nottingham

Dogs

The fast, the slim,
The slow, the fat,
Mongrels, pedigrees
All sorts of dogs.
Greyhounds are fast
They run around,
Sometimes they are
Not to be found.
They like to run,
To run all day,
And what they like best
Is to play!
Bulldogs are big,
Bold and fat
They don't like to run
Just sit on the mat.
Some say they're ugly
And very slow,
They're quite wide
And like to show.
Spaniels are cute
And really nice,
They're quite fast
And can catch mice.
They like the water
And go very deep
When they come out
They go to sleep!

Eve Birkin (10)
Fernwood Junior School, Nottingham

The Park At Night

The night is coming, fast and quick
Birds retreating, small and slick.
I saunter along, looking around
Listening hard, not hearing a sound.
This night is black, dark and creepy
Now I'm anything but sleepy.
The moon is shining, climbing the sky
I quicken my pace, my fear's high.
I don't want to see the dark anymore
I turn on my torch and there's white galore.
Ghosts, ghouls, skulls and scares
All the creatures from nightmares.
Gathered together in the dark
Of the haunted, scary park.
They're closing in on me,
Now I know I'll die,
Find this poem where I lie.

Ellie Bouttell (10)
Fernwood Junior School, Nottingham

The Chase

Hiding in the trees
Feeling the chilling breeze,
Wait!
It sees something.
Eye it!
Spy it!
Run and pounce.
Stop!
Eye it!
Spy it!
Run and pounce.
Catch it!
Miaow!
Tweet!
Splat!

Jessica Fitzgerald (10)
Fernwood Junior School, Nottingham

My Family

I've got two sisters, Lara and Becca
Who want to be queens.
A mother who wants to be a childminder
And a dad that thinks he's a footballer
And of course, me.
But I'm different
I just want to be . . .
Me!

Jessica Bailey (10)
Fernwood Junior School, Nottingham

My Bedroom Isn't Big

My bedroom isn't big but it isn't small
And it's not square-shaped or circular
In fact there's not much there at all.
There's a bed in the corner
And some drawers at the back
And a table in the middle
So how about that!
There are some photos on the wall
Of my sister, mum and dad
And a big one on the table
Of me looking mad.
There's a pile of books at the back of my bed
Of fairy tales and dreamers
Which I haven't yet read
And I just want to say
I think my bedroom's the best from everywhere
East, north, south and west.

Ellie Gorski (10)
Fernwood Junior School, Nottingham

I Want!

A sip of sparkling squash
Chips, chocolate and cake
I want to have all this food
I don't want it to be fake.

A terrific, talking teddy
To get to stay in bed
A posh, perfect pony
A furry flamingo that's red!

A jungle in my sitting room
A forest by my bath
A cave in my kitchen
A lion that's called Cath!

Please give me all these things
I want them to be true
Tell me if you've got them
Or give me some kind of clue.

Hattie Clark (9)
Fernwood Junior School, Nottingham

My Cat

My cat called Pop is gorgeous
She likes to laze on my bed
She loves to play with string
And she is very well fed.

Pop is three colours, black, brown and white
She hates my other cat, Fizz
So she likes to get in a fight.

Becky Webster (9)
Fernwood Junior School, Nottingham

Stampede!

Elephants stomping
Buffalo bumping
Zebra charging
Rhinos barging
Antelope leaping
Cheetah cheating
Herons squawking
Parrots talking
All in the big stampede.

Joseph Nowicki (9)
Fernwood Junior School, Nottingham

Colours

C olours all around you
O live-green with a red hat on top
L ight blue like the clear blue sky
O range in your clothes, orange that you eat
U nited States colours, dark blue and dark red
R unning red blood, running down your cheeks
S unshine-yellow, yellow lemons.

Melissa Mahdavi (9)
Fernwood Junior School, Nottingham

Raindrops

When the raindrops fall
They look like tiny drops of ice
A shattered window.

Francesca McDonald (10)
Fernwood Junior School, Nottingham

Cheetah - Haiku

There goes the cheetah
Running, gliding through the grass
Like a bird soaring.

Danielle Page (9)
Fernwood Junior School, Nottingham

In My Dreams

In my dreams I am
A small red ladybird
And I have a nap.

Frances Cripps (10)
Fernwood Junior School, Nottingham

Fish - Haiku

The fish are swimming
In their underwater den
A thousand petals.

Kate Hetmanski (10)
Fernwood Junior School, Nottingham

Fish

Fish are swimming around
In their own little den
Like small skittles in water.

Annie McCoy (10)
Fernwood Junior School, Nottingham

Fire

Dangerous he is as he storms through trees
Like a tiger he runs
Like a monkey he climbs
Ever burning
Everything bows down to his merciless claws
Until his anger ceases
He fades away
Receding to a calming presence
He flickers inside a stone cage
And he cuddles close to
Any living thing
To warm their hearts.

Ryan McGrath (10)
Fernwood Junior School, Nottingham

My Parrot

My parrot's called Lenny
He squawks all day
I'm glad we get peace at night.

He gets on my nerves
I don't know why
But it never gives me a headache.

My friends always say,
'Oh my ears,
That awful parrot!'

But I think that's horrible
I love my parrot
And no one can change my mind.

Hannah Horsewill (10)
Fernwood Junior School, Nottingham

Mr Pink

Mr Pink is small
He's always having a brawl
Adam is his brother
Who likes going shopping with his mother.

Mr pink likes football
He hates everyone who doesn't like it at all
Trace is his dad
Who's not that very mad.

Mr Pink likes pink
He likes it better than a wink
Lorraine is his mother
They like to play games with each other.

Josh Taylor (9)
Fernwood Junior School, Nottingham

My Funny Pet

My pet is a funny thing
He jumps and wags his tail
He begs for some meaty treats
And never wants to fail.

And if you have a race with him
You're guaranteed to fail
If you put a thing in front
You know what's gonna happen
Snap!

Adam Fox (10)
Fernwood Junior School, Nottingham

Guess?

Chewing, biting
Never fighting
Cute 'n' nice
Wouldn't hurt mice
Plain colours
But never gets duller
Guessed what it is yet?
It's easy to get!
No? OK . . .
Not good at croquet
Nor at dancing
No way is it prancing
Black 'n' white
That's right -
Pandas!

Chloe Thompson (9)
Fernwood Junior School, Nottingham

The Wolf

The wolf streaks after its prey
A blurry, browny grey.

The terrible hunter
The bone cruncher.
The meat-eating monster
Getting closer and closer.
It's after the mice
It's not very nice.

It then pounces on the helpless mouse
And then it joins the lonely woodlouse,
Inside the monster's stomach.

Charlotte Smith (10)
Fernwood Junior School, Nottingham

My Weird Family

My brother is a Martian
He comes from outer space
You don't need to ask him
Just look at his face.

My auntie is a devil
She's haunted my house for years
She howls like a wolf in the night
But no one ever hears.

My brother's face is ugly
He's also very green
His ears are as big as a pussycat
And his features are very mean.

She creeps about in the night
Tickling people's ears
She is a phantom spelling test failer
She's been like that for years.

He has bulging biceps
They're bigger than a dog
I am only lying really
They're bigger than a log!

Tim Freeman (10)
Fernwood Junior School, Nottingham

On My Desk!

MP3, old CD
Old Game Boy, rusty toy
Yu-Gi-Oh box, plastic fox
Sweet packet, broken racket
Rubbish bin, hammered pin
Strings on a guitar, mini car
Pizza slice, baby mice
1p, pitcher of the sea
Tub of ice cream, hero team
All sitting on the top of my desk!

Joel Dudley (8)
Fernwood Junior School, Nottingham

Haiku

The river flowing
The red rocks in the water
Fishes in a row.

Asif Mehmood (10)
Fernwood Junior School, Nottingham

Under The Bed

Sweet packet, broken racket
Small 1p, rusty key
Mobile phone, ice cream cone
Old toothbrush, Mum's make-up brush
Dad's favourite book, picture of a cook
Broken frame, T-shirt with a stain
Toy hamster, magnet gangster
Dead bird, picture of a nerd
Piece of candy, doll called Mandy
An old ted, almost forgotten under the bed.

Raul Ladwa (8)
Fernwood Junior School, Nottingham

Gymnastics - Haikus

I love gymnastics
I really love gymnastics
Bridge, splits, handstand too.

On the big playground
Making up a dance routine
With cartwheels in it.

Time to do our work
Back in the classroom, boring
Playtime now again.

Hannah Clay (9)
Fernwood Junior School, Nottingham

On My Bedroom Floor

On my bedroom floor you would find . . .

Mrs Cox,
A green box
A golden fox
Wearing smelly socks.

A Jack-in-a-box, *boo!*
A black shoe
A doll who says who
So I say, 'Phew!'

A red car
A chocolate bar
Half-eaten so far.

Two Jacqueline Wilson books
Ten wooden hooks
A lion who gives you looks.

On my bedroom floor you would smell . . .

Big wooden arks
Full of blood hearts
Little mini frogs
The smelly smell of logs.

Afnan Dridi (8)
Fernwood Junior School, Nottingham

Daisy-May

Fish nibbler
Curtain runner
That's our Daisy-May

Mouse terroriser
Fur leaver
That's our Daisy-May

Scratcher snatcher
Noisy nuisance
That's our Daisy-May.

She runs round our hall and up our stairs
I wonder how she dares
That's our Daisy-May!

Rebecca Godbeer (10)
Fernwood Junior School, Nottingham

Frustration

Frustration is not being able to do a sum
Frustration is not being able to do your work
Frustration is not being able to do a jigsaw
Frustration is not being able to pick your nose
Frustration is not being able to pick up your last pea on your plate
Frustration is not being able to tidy your room
Frustration is not being able to write
Frustration is not being able to read a book
Frustration is not being able to do your work in time.

Kishan Patel (9)
Fernwood Junior School, Nottingham

Sadness

Sadness is someone who has died
Sadness is losing a football match
Sadness is losing a pet
Sadness is breaking a toy
Sadness is trapping your finger in the door.

Myles Smith (9)
Fernwood Junior School, Nottingham

Happiness

Happiness is when you get a puppy and you feel happy
Happiness is when you are happy when you meet new friends
Happiness is when you eat all your dinner
Happiness is when you have a good giggle
Happiness is when you get a sticker
Happiness is when your tooth falls out
Happiness is when we do art
Happiness is when our teacher doesn't tell us off
Happiness is when you get a Tracy Beaker DVD.

Lauren Williams (9)
Fernwood Junior School, Nottingham

Shopping

Pink skirts, white shirts
Yellow slippers, chicken dippers
Baked beans, blue jeans
Shepherd's pie, hair dye
Orange juice, chocolate mousse
Sour lemon, juicy melon
Denim jackets, crisp packets
Chocolate spread, homemade bread
Toy mole, sausage roll
Chocolate bar, pink bra
Olive oil, silver foil
Waistcoat, plastic boat
Chocolate mice, white rice.

Lydia Miah (9)
Fernwood Junior School, Nottingham

Museums

Dinosaur bones, royal thrones
Egyptian mummies, historical dummies
Dusty books, mummified ducks
Aboriginal art, Picasso art
Egyptian cat, Persian mat
A majestic crown, Japanese gown.

Daniel Roshanmoniri (9)
Fernwood Junior School, Nottingham

Sadness

Sadness is when you lose a pet
Sadness is when someone passes away
Sadness is when you can't see a friend
Sadness is when you are ill
Sadness is when you die
Sadness is when you have a detention
Sadness is when you don't do your homework
Sadness is when your writing is not neat
Sadness is when you are told off
Sadness is when you can't do something
Sadness is when you can't see your parents
Sadness is when you can't do it anymore
Sadness is when you can't explain when you're told off
Sadness is when you get picked on.

Gurdas Swali (9)
Fernwood Junior School, Nottingham

A Football Match - Haiku

Scoring a free kick
The final whistle has gone
Lifting the trophy.

Amran Nagra (9)
Fernwood Junior School, Nottingham

Happiness

Happiness is a new bike
Happiness is a new job
Happiness is doing a performance
Happiness is losing a tooth
Happiness is making a friend
Happiness is turning eighteen
Happiness is leaving school.

Holly Sherriff (8)
Fernwood Junior School, Nottingham

Girl's Bedroom

Brand new bed for my head
Lovely light for the night
Old book, plastic ducks
Pink shirt, yellow skirt
Worn out slipper, light flickers
Dusty floor, white door
Dirty boot, silver flute
Red teddy, I'm ready
Blue top, can of pop
Pink bobble, my hair wobbles
Fluffy pen, model hen.

Claire Bennett (9)
Fernwood Junior School, Nottingham

My Fish Goldy

She's as orange as the sun
As big as a computer mouse
Scales like little sequins
Stones and plants in her house.

Fun, sparkly and smooth
Fast, speedy and smelly
Friendly, energetic and beautiful
She eats lots of food and she's got a big belly.

Swimming up and down
Left, round, right, turn, swish
Round the corner a splash all around
It's Goldy, my pet fish!

Sophie Bee (10)
Fernwood Junior School, Nottingham

Chipmunk

I   a
Chipmunk?
Small, furry,
I'm one!
  A pet?
   Me? Very rare! Me? A pet? I don't care!
  You don't often see a chipmunk in a pet shop!
  I bet no one's going to buy me in a place like here.
   Tiny animal, small not cuddly, brown usually.
      I, a chipmunk   small, furry, I'm one.
    A pet? Me?   Very rare? Me? A pet?
    I don't care! Now I'm being looked at, I don't know why.
Now I know I'm being bought! Here at the counter I am being bought.
Yippee! How wonderful it is to be someone's pet, I, a chipmunk?
  Small, furry, I'm one! A pet? Me? Very rare! Me? A pet?

               I am!

Caroline Jones (9)
Fernwood Junior School, Nottingham

The Graveyard

G raves are everywhere surrounding me like an army of men
  ambushing me

R ain is dropping on the solid, marble gravestones, drip-drop!

A ll I can see is a grey, dull mist, brushing the grass with its gentle
  touch

V illagers come to pray that their loved ones are safe in Jesus' arms

E veryone comes to see their loved ones and bring flowers to put on
  their grave

Y ards are usually happy, fun places but this yard was not

A whole yard of grey graves, like a blanket of grey and dirty snow

R est in peace my friends, then rise again

D ead people are in their graves having a big rest, the last rest they
  will ever have.

Matthew Simpson (10)
Fernwood Junior School, Nottingham

Bushy Climber

Bushy tail
Active nail
Tree climber
Wind chimer
Branch hopper
Tree topper
Smart poser
Heavy dozer.

Edward Smith (10)
Fernwood Junior School, Nottingham

Happiness

Happiness is when you make friends together
Happiness is when you have a cute dog
Happiness is when you get a laptop
Happiness is when you get some money
Happiness is when you get good work
Happiness is when you lie in bed all day
Happiness is when you have a laugh
Happiness is when you play on your PS2
Happiness is when you go somewhere good
Happiness is when you have a birthday
Happiness is when you have a giggle
Happiness is when you win a football match
Happiness is when you get to go to a museum
Happiness is when you know your tables
Happiness is when you try Chinese food
Happiness is when you go shopping.

Lalit Sharma (9)
Fernwood Junior School, Nottingham

Happiness Is . . .

Happiness is when your dog comes home
Happiness is when your friend comes to your house
Happiness is when your dog has puppies
Happiness is going on holiday
Happiness is when you get a new friend
Happiness is coming out of a detention
Happiness is good work
Happiness is when your friend moves back to school.

Dana Ravenscroft (8)
Fernwood Junior School, Nottingham

Alphabet Poem

A is for Alice who bites her nails
B is for Bennie who picks lots of snails
C is for Claire who has a toy car
D is for Daniel who works in a bar
E is for Emily who loves lots of jelly
F is for Frank whose toes are smelly
G is for Georgia who is very sweet
H is for Henry who has lots of treats
I is for Isabella who is very moody
J is for Jack whose chicken is broody
K is for Kate who is very chubby
L is for Lydia who is very grubby
M is for Melanie who is very stroppy
N is for Ned who's ever so sloppy
O is for Olivia who's ever so kind
P is for Patrick who's nearly blind
Q is for Quentin who's always caring
R is for Rebecca who is always sharing
S is for Sam who's always naughty
T is for Tim who's turning forty
U is for Ugo who is very cute
V is for Vicky who has a big boat
W is for Wallace who is quite good
X is for Xavier who's covered in mud
Y is for Yasmin who is very pretty
Z is for Zac who has a kitty.

Parvinder Kaur (9)
Fernwood Junior School, Nottingham

Sweet Shop

Lollipop, stick of rock
Chocolate bar, Mars bar
A bar of Bounty, eaten at County
A strawberry cake, a chocolate Flake
Jelly bean, ice cream
A box of Smarties, eaten at parties
A packet of toffee, eaten with your coffee.

Reegan Morris (9)
Fernwood Junior School, Nottingham

Pete's Pets

In his room Pete kept . . .

Eight slimy slugs sliding on the window
Seven monkeys swinging on the lights
Six fat cats sleeping all day
Five kangaroos bouncing on the bed
Four elephants charging to and fro
Three tiny imps hiding from the kangaroo
Two long boa constrictors sliding all around
One . . . guess what?

James Cox (9)
Fernwood Junior School, Nottingham

Detention - Haiku

I hate detention
It is very horrible
I hate detention.

Shahryar Iravani (9)
Fernwood Junior School, Nottingham

Liverpool

Football dribbling
Across the pitch
Laces flicking up and down
Studs sticking in the ground.

Boots flicking up some mud
All the players are really good
Ball rolling all around
Sometimes up and hitting the ground.

Slide tackle coming in
Oh my gosh, a yellow card
Penalty coming up
Oh yes, what a goal!

They've won the FA Cup
There they are standing up
All have got smiles on their faces
What a match that was!

James Burrows (9)
Fernwood Junior School, Nottingham

Fairies Poem

I believe in fairies
Fairies live at the end of my bed
I believe that they come in my dreams
And a pea is the size of their head.

Flower and dream fairies
Live in anywhere you dream
I like fairy dreams
Because they make up fairy routines.

They flutter and fly over the blue sky
The fairies dance
With the violin and flute
And the fiddle that makes them prance.

Ruth Page (8)
Fernwood Junior School, Nottingham

Amar Is Going To Win!

'Amar's going to win!' I said
'No, he's not,' said Joel
'Is too!'
'Is not!'
'I bet you one pound, he's going to win!' I said.
'Deal!' agreed Joel.
'He's got wicked cards!'
'Has not!'
'He's won, I know it!' I told Joel.
'He's got rubbish cards!' shouted Joel.
Amar comes through the door.
'I've won!' he told everyone.
I went up to Joel,
'Hand over the money!'

Edward Hirst (9)
Fernwood Junior School, Nottingham

Kids, Kids And More . . . Kids

A is for Albert who has lots of toys
B is for Beth who loves to chase boys
C is for Charlie who eats quite a lot
D is for Dilbert who has a small cot
E is for Elizabeth who likes her walking
F is for Fred who does a lot of talking
G is for Glenda who's in love with Fred
H is for Harry who hates going to bed
I is for Isabelle who doesn't like cakes
J is for James who used to bake
K is for Kath who likes to sniff
L is for Lynda who called her dog Cliff
M is for Mandy who is quite a bully
N is for Noel who's the opposite and cuddly
O is for Orlando who is quite thick
P is for Paige, who in her bag you'll find a brick
Q is for Quinn who is very clever
R is for Russell who never says never
S is for Sam who eats lots of food
T is for Tom who can be quite rude
U is for Ursula who has always got a smile
V is for Van who's off for a while
W is for Walter who is very fat
X is for Xavier who has a pet bat
Y is for Ying Gring who is a fool
Z is for Zak who's got a pool.

Adam Russell (9)
Fernwood Junior School, Nottingham

Sound Collector

(Based on 'The Sound Collector' by Roger McGough)

A stranger called this morning
In a dark, dull colour
He took away the sounds
And put them in his bag.

The noise of the TV
The ticking of the clock
The rumbling of my mum's tummy
The dog's barking.

The microwave spinning
The crunching in my mouth
My dad's shouting
It was very loud.

The bubbling in the pan
The dripping of the tap
The refrigerator freezing
Me bouncing on the bed.

My brother's drumming
The tapping of my shoes
The washing machine
The drill drilling.

The baby crying
My dad breaking a chair
The gulping of the drains
And my brother sleeping.

The toilet being flushed
He didn't leave his name
He left our house quietly
It's not the same!

Bharath Sharma (9)
Fernwood Junior School, Nottingham

The River

The river is long and it twists in all different directions.
It creeps through forests and appears out of the blue.
It slithers over rocks and slowly glides on its way.

Hitting its obstacles it hisses angrily.
Nevertheless, when back on track, it's a silent breeze blowing gently.

After a lazy day in the sun,
The river takes a turn and it's out of control.
It swallows its prey whole and devours its food in one gigantic gulp,
Nothing can survive the river's bite!

Joanna Wallace (11)
St Werburgh's CE Primary School, Derby

Wonderful Chest

(Based on 'Magic Box' by Kit Wright)

I will put in my chest . . .
The horn of a bull lost in battle.
The taste of lightning in an offensive storm.
A witch's spell of tittle-tattle.
The smile of a twisty worm.

I will put in my chest . . .
The first sense of roses on a dusky dawn.
The honesty of a wise old man.
The vivid green of a dew-covered lawn.
The tender knees of a newborn lamb.

I will put in my chest . . .
A cart before a horse.
The thirteenth month.
A racing car course
And the responsibility of an older sister.

Lauren Collings (11)
St Werburgh's CE Primary School, Derby

My Best Friend

You're the soft petal on my large flower.
You're the flickering candle on my chocolate cake.
You're the closed corners on my square
To seal all the secrets that I make.

You're the fast whizz in my life.
You're the beaming sun in my sky.
You're the fluffy tissue who's always by my side
To cheer me up when I cry.

You're the singing choir in the village hall
With a voice of a sweet angel.
You're the tender smoked salmon
In my hot, luxurious bagel.

You're the best ever friend
In the whole entire Earth.
Your deluxe white wings
Must have been given at birth.

You're the best ever friend
I'll never forget you.

Kirsty Fazekas (11)
St Werburgh's CE Primary School, Derby

My Magic Pot

(Based on 'Magic Box' by Kit Wright)

I will put in my pot . . .
The feather of a dove,
The shine from the sun
And the taste of a freshly baked breadcrumb bun.

I will put in my pot . . .
The scent from a flower,
The touch of grass
And the view of a ship with a beautiful mast.

I will put in my pot . . .
The comfort from my duvet,
The touch of silk
And the beautiful taste of freshly cooled milk.

I will put in my pot . . .
The sound of a bird,
The voice of a choir,
I will put in my pot whatever I desire.

Ben Knapp (10)
St Werburgh's CE Primary School, Derby

Bird In The Tree

Bird in the tree
What do you see?
A lawnmower whizzing towards a tall tree,
A flower attracting a bee,
In the overgrown grass, a glittering, lost, golden key,
On the table, a cup of cold herbal tea.

Bird in the tree,
What do you smell?
The brassy smell of the ringing bell,
The fresh water dripping into a well,
The leafy aroma of nature's gel,
The mustiness of a bedroom from an open window, just like a
                                                    prison cell.

Bird in the tree,
What do you hear?
A little mouse scurrying away from a cat, filled with fear.
The cat growls as it comes ever so near,
And a dog gives a barking jeer,
As the cat comes close, while the mouse lets out a safe little cheer.

Katie Pealing (10)
St Werburgh's CE Primary School, Derby

Snail On The Window

What can you hear?
The screech of a van,
The flickering of a lamp post,
The siren of a police car,
The shouting of teenagers,
A baby screaming like a bat.

What else can you hear?
The shout of children playing,
The whistle of a robin,
The cheer of a crowd,
The buzzing of a bee
A mother humming like a bird.

Alex Revill (11)
St Werburgh's CE Primary School, Derby

Up Above

You're the very hot sun
That blazes on and on.
You're the amazing powerful fireball
That is extremely, extremely hot.

You're the magnificent Earth
That God has created.
You're the blue and green spherical planet
That is third in the solar system.

You're the splendid Pluto
That is cold and small.
You're the blue cold planet
That is last in the rhyme.

You're the whole of the up above
That means the planets and the sun.
You're the stars and the moon,
You're all of the up above.

Kirsten Fooks (10)
St Werburgh's CE Primary School, Derby

Calming Leaf

A smooth red leaf swings from a tree
A gust of cool wind
Propelling it onwards,
It travels softly forwards
Landing on the rough ground.

The rough feel of snakeskin
Brushes its back,
As it lays down to rest
And closes its sharp eyes.

Grace Gillam (10)
St Werburgh's CE Primary School, Derby

My Special Chest

(Based on 'Magic Box' by Kit Wright)

I will put in my chest . . .
The softness of the multicoloured rainbow,
The fluffiness of clouds
And the brightness of the daylight.

I will put in my chest . . .
The sound of trickling streams,
The roughness of the tree trunks
And the heat from the fiery sun.

Joe Wreford (10)
St Werburgh's CE Primary School, Derby

My Special Pot

(Based on 'Magic Box' by Kit Wright)

I will put in my pot . . .
The murmur of the wind,
The song of the trees,
The wonders of the rainbow
And the dancing of the honeybees.

I will put in my pot . . .
A sun covered in gilt,
A fluffy cloud that covered the sky,
The magic of love
And a jewel from up high.

My pot holds treasures far greater than the king's,
Greater secrets than the queen's
More precious than a magic spell,
More powerful than a magic bean.

Tess Clark (10)
St Werburgh's CE Primary School, Derby

My Family

You're the bones in my body that support me,
You're the newest daffodil in the awakening spring,
You're the smoothest of the newly made silk,
You're the sweetest smelling scent in the whole wide world,
You are the sun on a cloudy day that shines through the clouds,
You're the melting cheese in my mouth as I bite the newly made pizza,
You're the pot of gold at the end of the glimmering rainbow
That shines so brightly on a gloomy day,
You're the biggest diamond in the world that glimmers brightly in the
radiant sun.

Thomas Fearn-Wright (11)
St Werburgh's CE Primary School, Derby

My Family

You are the sun on a summer day,
You are my muscles that give me strength,
You are the breeze that brushes against me when I need you,
You are the brightest colours in the world,
You're the chocolate that melts in my mouth,
You're the sweetest smell in the whole of the galaxy,
You are fantastic,
You are my family.

Liam Slaney (11)
St Werburgh's CE Primary School, Derby

Bird

I wish I were a bird
I could fly away to sea,
See what people are doing
Whatever it may be.

I wish I were a bird
I could watch football for free,
Get a bird's-eye view of the game
And then go home for tea!

I wish I were a bird
I'd fly to catch prey,
I could fly away from predators
Fly far away.

I wish I were a bird
With beautiful long wings,
But now I come to think of it
I can do most of these things.

Joe Wood (11)
St Werburgh's CE Primary School, Derby

The Supernatural Bag

(Based on 'Magic Box' by Kit Wright)

I will put in the bag . . .
The whispering wind on my face,
The sun's powerful light illuminating the Earth,
The beautiful song of a bird in a tree.

I will put in the bag . . .
The soft pattering of the rain on the roof,
The moon's magnificent shine,
The soft touch of a flower petal.

I will put in the bag . . .
The feeling of the damp dew-covered lawn,
The taste of early morning air,
A flowing river, stretching out to a glistening sea.

I will put in the bag . . .
A monkey's squeal,
An elephant's stomp
And a mouse's shrill squeak.

My supernatural bag is made of the finest oakwood,
Polished until shiny, encrusted with diamonds with a fine gold lock.

Sam Wreford (10)
St Werburgh's CE Primary School, Derby

My Special Chest

(Based on 'Magic Box' by Kit Wright)

I will put in my chest . . .
The different shapes and sizes of the bright shining stars,
The wonderful colours of the never-ending rainbow,
And the white fluffy feeling of a cloud in the blue sky.

I will put in my chest . . .
The magic of flowing water as it runs down the river,
The sight of a beautiful blackbird flying high in the air
And the wide variety of crunchy leaves on a tree.

I will put in my chest . . .
The feeling of rough yellow sand as it rushes through your hands,
The sound of the tick on a dark brown grandfather clock
And the coldness of a winter breeze as it blows your hair.

Ben Taylor (11)
St Werburgh's CE Primary School, Derby

Excitement

Excitement is orange like my favourite jelly wobbling on my spoon.
Excitement smells like a chocolate bar about to be eaten.
Excitement tastes like fizzy lemonade as it bubbles in my throat.
Excitement feels like butterflies in my tummy.
Excitement looks like a pile of presents waiting to be opened.
Excitement sounds like fireworks crashing through the night air.
Excitement reminds me of holidays, Christmas and birthdays.

Amy Harvey (10)
St Werburgh's CE Primary School, Derby

Favourite Things

You're an old sunflower
Facing the sun, bright and bold,
Your skin is soft silk of the finest quality.

You're a bright sun
Shining over a soft shimmering sea,
Drifting through the air, helping people on their way.

You're the soft sand
On a Mediterranean beach,
Smooth and soft for your loved one to walk on.

Some people say you're a guardian to help us,
You're my mum!

Abigail Anderson (10)
St Werburgh's CE Primary School, Derby

Can I Do The Impossible?

Can I touch the rainbow that will feel smooth on the side?
Can I tip the world upside down to see if gravity is real?
Can I grow wings so I can fly and soar through the air?
Can I have magic powers to make a happier life?
Can I have a pet dragon to fight in battles?
Can I sleep on a cloud and drift through the sky?
Can I paint a picture with money to make it priceless?
Can I jump up and catch a star to see it shine in my eyes?
Can I go back in time to demolish all the bad things?
Can I do these impossibles or are they just my dreams?

Bronte Owen (10)
St Werburgh's CE Primary School, Derby

The Black Stallion

As black as night,
As strong as steel,
The pure black pony gallops
Along the beach,
Over the hills,
He comforts the stray and injured.

Covering the ground like a calm, graceful sea
His mane glitters softly in the breeze,
Jumping hedges,
Jumping streams,
He breaks the stillness with his shrill whinnying.

As black as night,
As strong as steel,
The pure black pony gallops.

Katie Roethenbaugh (10)
St Werburgh's CE Primary School, Derby

Happiness

Happiness is like going on holiday near the sea with the blazing sun.
It feels like walking on a cloud in total silence.
It reminds me of the happiest time of my life.
It sounds like birds in the morning chirping.
It tastes like sweets and candy canes.
The colours yellow, blue and green because they are all colours of happiness.

Joshua Large (10)
St Werburgh's CE Primary School, Derby

Frog In A Pond, What Do You Hear?

A cat slinking across the freshly-mowed lawn,
The rain bouncing off the glassy surface of the pond,
A man humming softly as he spots the dawn breaking through the
mist.
A mouse sneaking under some tree roots,
The sun beating down onto the ground,
A girl struggling to pull on her boots.
A grasshopper playing music on its back feet,
The creatures hidden among the grass droning continuously
A honeybee cavorting around some wheat.
These are all the things I can hear.

Bethany Marshall (10)
St Werburgh's CE Primary School, Derby

Love

Love is like the first colour in the rainbow.
It feels like a smooth piece of felt.
It looks like a ripe tomato.
It smells of soft ketchup.
It sounds like the calm wind.
It tastes like a sweet strawberry.
It reminds me of my friends and family.

Amy Stephenson (8)
St Werburgh's CE Primary School, Derby

Love

Love is red like a new sweet strawberry.
It feels as soft as puppy fur.
It smells like super perfume.
It sounds like a quiet whisper.
It tastes like crisps in my tummy.

Danielle Harvey (8)
St Werburgh's CE Primary School, Derby

The Secret Place

I've found a secret place
There's only room for me,
It's tucked up hidden in my bedroom
I've even got a key.

My sister tries to follow me
Up to my bedroom,
This is how I scare her away
Saying it's a haunted little tomb.

I love my little secret place
Where there's only room for me,
But I'm afraid I have to leave my room
Because I can smell my tea.

Ellie Hill (9)
St Werburgh's CE Primary School, Derby

Love

Love is red like shiny roses.
It smells like fresh poppies in the morning fields.
It sounds like your heart is beating fast.
It tastes like fresh morning snow.
It feels like a smooth shell on the beach.
It reminds you of your first kiss.

Idony Baker-Hodkinson (8)
St Werburgh's CE Primary School, Derby

War And Peace

War filled with hatred,
Screaming to the sound of bombs,
Stomping to endless anger,
Erupting with fear to scare away everyone in its path!

Peace filled with joy and laughter,
Treading carefully towards shelter,
Singing to the sounding of love and the glistening moon,
Erupting with joy, love and laughter
Laugher has risen again.

Jordan Cook (11)
St Werburgh's CE Primary School, Derby

Please

(Based on 'Please Mrs Butler' by Allan Ahlberg)

'Please Mr Bigbolt
This boy Jack Jolt
Keeps nudging my pen
What shall I do?'

'Go and sit in the toilet dear
Take your stuff to the grounds
Go to the hall
Just do whatever you want at all.'

'Please Mr Bigbolt
This boy Jack Jolt
Keeps poking me in the head
What shall I do?'

'Lock yourself in the drawer
Sit in the sink,
Hide behind a tree
Just leave me be!'

Dylan Mahowa (11)
St Werburgh's CE Primary School, Derby

Anger

Anger is grey as the raining clouds.
It feels like a hard stone.
It sounds like a pounding drum.
It looks like a burning flame.
It smells like dark smoke and tastes like a sour lemon.

Kyle Weeks (9)
St Werburgh's CE Primary School, Derby

Football

Football is great
Play with your mate
Have a dream
About playing for your favourite team.

Football is great
You don't gain weight
The pitch is green
Eat a baked bean.

Joshua Cook (11)
St Werburgh's CE Primary School, Derby

Have You Got A Chocolate Bar?

Have you got a chocolate bar?
Can I have a bite?
Can I have a big fat chunk
Or even a little bite?

Can I have a bit of it
Please, a little crumb?
I need a little chocolate
It makes me really fun.

I hope you haven't eaten it all,
Been a big, greedy pig.
I really, really want a bit
Oh no! You ate it all!

Ryan Fayers (10)
St Werburgh's CE Primary School, Derby

Anger

Anger feels like a brick smashing against the wall.
It smells like a soggy banana.
It sounds like cymbals crashing together.
It tastes like a red-hot fire.
Anger reminds me of the Devil hanging over you.
It looks like a bomb exploding.

Jamie Baker (11)
St Werburgh's CE Primary School, Derby

Spring

Spring is colourful
Past goes the ice cream van
Ring goes the church bells
Inside goes the winter
No more hibernating
Going on holiday, spring is great.

Benjamin Wilford (11)
St Werburgh's CE Primary School, Derby

Love

Love is red like a petal of a rose.
Love smells like perfume in a spray can.
Love tastes like a Galaxy Caramel melting in your mouth.
Love reminds me of chocolate.
Love feels like a lovely hot bath.

Corey Moore (8)
St Werburgh's CE Primary School, Derby

On Holiday

When I go on holiday
It's always somewhere warm,
All I hope is at night there isn't a storm.
No matter how I try, I just can't get to sleep
And when I have to get up I'm always in a heap!

When I go on holiday
There's always different food to eat,
Whether it be vegetable or exotic meat.
All I smell is clean fresh air
But when we get home I say it isn't fair.

Kieran Truby-Ware (10)
St Werburgh's CE Primary School, Derby

My Special Box

(Based on 'Magic Box' by Kit Wright)

I will put in my box . . .
The waves on the open sea,
The shine of the sun on a hot summer day
And the beauty of the planets high in the sky.

I will put in my box . . .
The colours of a rainbow,
The sound of roaring thunder
And the feel of a lion's furry coat.

I will put in my box . . .
A north-west breeze rushing through my hair,
A stained glass window filled with colours beyond belief
And the scent of a million new bud roses.

I will put in my box . . .,
The burning fire from a volcano,
Diamonds and emeralds from the depth of a cave
And a nightingale singing sweetly at the top of its voice.

Richard Allen (11)
St Werburgh's CE Primary School, Derby

Love

Love is red like roses in the beautiful grass.
It feels so soft like sheep's cuddly wool.
It sounds quiet like only a whisper.
It smells lush like perfume on my mum's neck.
It tastes smooth like delicious melted chocolate.

Liam Marshall (8)
St Werburgh's CE Primary School, Derby

Anger

Anger is grey like the dark, spooky rain clouds.
Anger is rough like scratchy sandpaper.
Anger is smelly just like an old boot.
Anger is loud like a booming beam of thunder.
Anger is strong like a tube of salt.
Anger reminds me of my mum and brother
Who are always getting angry with each other.

Katy Birch (8)
St Werburgh's CE Primary School, Derby

Love

Love is bright red like roses in soil.
It feels soft like kitten's fur.
Love smells like a new burning fire and tastes like ice cream fresh from the freezer.
It sounds like the gentle wind and reminds me of Valentine's Day
So that's love!

Ellie Beech (8)
St Werburgh's CE Primary School, Derby

Hunger

Hunger is red like a shiny strawberry.
It feels empty like a dry swimming pool.
It smells like chips frying in a pan.
It tastes like saltwater from the blue ocean.
It sounds like a drum beating my tummy.

Ethan Beardsley (8)
St Werburgh's CE Primary School, Derby

Happiness

Happiness is pink like some roses in the park.
It feels like a woolly sheep.
It tastes like candyfloss.
It smells like a basket of apples.
It looks like a smiling person.
It sounds like a laughing person.
It reminds me of a freshly made sweet.
So that's what happiness is.

Becky Reeves (8)
St Werburgh's CE Primary School, Derby

Fear

Fear is black, as dark as the night sky.
Fear is hard, as tough as stone.
Fear is loud, as high-pitched as screeching.
Fear is stinky, as smelly as an old boot.
Fear is yucky and as bad-tasting as rotten bananas.
Fear is scary; it reminds me of a vampire.

Alex Nicholls (8)
St Werburgh's CE Primary School, Derby

Love

Love is red like the heart in your body.
It's so soft like a puppy's fur.
Love is sweet like crystal-white sugar.
Love is about being with each other and never letting it stop.

Ella O'Neill (8)
St Werburgh's CE Primary School, Derby

Love

It looks as red as running blood inside your scaly skin.
It feels like a big, furry bear sitting in the zoo.
It smells like a fresh summer meadow.
It tastes like candy pink and blue.
It sounds like wind whistling in the sun.
Now that's love.

Chloe Oxley (7)
St Werburgh's CE Primary School, Derby

The Love Poem

Love is red like a roaring fire.
It's so soft like a feather.
Love has a beautiful sound like church bells ringing all day long.
Love reminds me of beautiful hearts.
It smells like fresh roses in the morning.
And it tastes so sweet, like sugar.

Jake Stoddart (8)
St Werburgh's CE Primary School, Derby

My Friend

You're the smile on my face that keeps me going.
You're the sun shining brightly in the morning sky.
You're the energy in my body that makes me positive.
You're the heart of my soul gliding through the breeze.
You're the colours in the sky, without you the world would be dark and
gloomy.
You're the sun keeping away the mist and wind.
You're like a force-field to keep away the bad.
You're the person who keeps birds singing their beautiful songs.
You're the music of what the grass dances to in the morning breeze.
You're the best thing that ever happened to me.

Saul Shields (10)
St Werburgh's CE Primary School, Derby

Love

Love is red like a beautiful rose.
It feels so smooth, like a stone.
It sounds like a twittering in the air.
It smells like some refreshing perfume.
It tastes like a sweet strawberry.
It reminds me of loving my family.

Laura Milner (8)
St Werburgh's CE Primary School, Derby

Love

Love is as red as a bright heart.
Love is as soft as sheep's wool.
It looks so bright in the light blue sky.
It smells as hot as the sun in the sky.
It sounds as loud as a big beating heart.
It tastes as sweet as the sweets in the shop.
Love reminds me of a sweet violin.
Love feels like a soft, sweet heart.

Natasha Marshall (8)
St Werburgh's CE Primary School, Derby

The Highway Skater

(Based on 'The Highwayman' by Alfred Noyes)

The wind was a cluster of darkness,
The moon was the brightest star,
The road was like a ridged crisp
And the highway skater came skating, skating, skating
The highway skater came skating up to the skate shop.

Slowly the skater picked up his skateboard
And walked into the shop
And was buying, buying, buying from the manager.

He'd a caped Quicksilver beanie on his head,
A black O'Neil canvas belt,
A dark red Vans hoody
A pair of Vans Floyd shoes,
A Sharp GX10 phone and a Quicksilver T-shirt.

And in the dark, riding to the pub
He walked in
Someone grabbed him
Chucked him outside then shot him.

Dan French (9)
Silverstone CE Junior School, Towcester

Untitled

I climbed the ominous stairway
Along the eerie hall,
And gazed up at the photographs
Hanging on the wall.

The windows so grimy and decaying
Seemed unkempt to me,
They glared out at an appalling view
Across the neglected lea.

My heart felt anxious and timid,
My thoughts with panic ran wild,
Returning to that lifeless house
I first knew as a child.

Philippa Sutton (11)
Silverstone CE Junior School, Towcester

The Indian Man

(Based on 'The Highwayman' by Alfred Noyes)

He had a green coat with golden patterns and golden cord
Around the edges of his coat.
He wore tight white trousers with black boots up to his knees,
And a white shirt with golden buttons.
He rode through the mist and struggling through the old oak branches,
He saw seven horses standing in a line by the old deserted circus,
He was wondering what was going on.
He rode faster and faster, getting closer and closer to the old deserted
circus,
The Indian man came riding, riding, riding.
He got to the old, deserted circus.
He saw a figure in the mist with shiny, long, black hair blowing in the
wind.
There were seven more figures around her,
With rifle guns, and one of the seven men had his rifle gun pointing to
her.
The Indian man got off his horse and picked up his gun and quickly
shot him in the mist.
The other six men started firing at the Indian man.
He ran towards the lady, untied the rope and grabbed her hand and
ran to the horse,
They rode far, far away and kept on riding, riding, riding.

Evie Dibble (10)
Silverstone CE Junior School, Towcester

Night Rider

(Based on 'the Highwayman' by Alfred Noyes)

The wind was a tree-lifting gale,
The moon was a crystal shining far away,
The road was a black coal trench
And the boneshaking madman came riding, riding, riding
Up to the deserted coal mine.

A skull for a head and flames for hair with a trail of flaming oil
The cape waving in the wind
A pistol on his bike ready to strike.
He was not alone, he was being watched and he knew it.
Then he drew his pistol, stopped his bike and shouted out, 'Come and fight'
The pistol loaded, he shot a bullet and hit his target.

Fire in the opposite direction,
He chased a mysterious figure driving a truck,
The figure had a hooded cape, black mask
And leather jacket with spikes down the arms.
Then he pulled out a shotgun and fired, fired, fired.
And the boneshaking madman turned, skidded, fell off, lost his pistol
And looked up to see the figure holding a blue chainsaw and that was the last he saw.

Jack Shaw (10)
Silverstone CE Junior School, Towcester

The Screamer

(Based on 'The Highwayman' by Alfred Noyes)

The wind was a freezing cold hurricane with icy sparks,
The moon was a pure white planet of secrets with a glittering glow,
The road was a straight cobble line with lots of memories,
Then the screamer came swooping, swooping, swooping
And the screamer came swooping up to the Victorian castle.

He'd a long black cape made of the finest velvet,
A pair of black tights under boots made of red leather.
He looked over the misty fields and pinched his cold, icy hand.
His shocking blue eyes scanned the misty land.
He saw a black as coal silhouette of a person
And he went soaring, soaring, soaring.
The screamer went soaring up into the air.

He was an arrow coming down straight to the silhouette,
Opening his mouth, showing pure white fangs.
His cape went from side to side
And the screamer went screaming, screaming, screaming.
The screamer went screaming and ate the person alive.

The army went charging in the misty moonlight,
Stamp, stamp, stamp went the army as they surrounded the screamer.
Stamp, stamp, stamp as the screamer went down,
No more death of innocent people.

Megan Goodman (10)
Silverstone CE Junior School, Towcester

The Ghost Rider

(Based on 'The Highwayman' by Alfred Noyes)

The wind was a stormy roar,
The moon was a silver planet,
The road was a stream of tar
And the ghost rider came floating, floating, floating,
The ghost rider came floating up to the abandoned railway station.

He'd an army cap on his forehead,
A uniform of medals, all swamp-green in colour and his trousers too!
His boots were pitch-black!
He held his sword in the air
And he got to the door of the station
He knocked it right down.

Somewhere in the station, a door creaked slowly opened and out of it
came a visitor,
Tom, the old historian, saw the ghost rider dismount and the ghost
rider came
Hovering, hovering, hovering,
The ghost rider came hovering to the ticket office.
Tom looked round and saw him, a truly terrible sight
But suddenly the ghost squad came charging down the door!

Toby Dennison (9)
Silverstone CE Junior School, Towcester

The Old Traveller's Inn

(Based on 'The Highwayman' by Alfred Noyes)

The wind was a howling monster,
The moon was a bright, light face,
The road was a very dusty pathway,
And the traveller came riding, riding, riding,
The traveller came riding up to the old dusty place.

He had an old hay hat
And a coat that was very dirty indeed,
He was wearing a pair of shorts that had lots of holes in
And they only came down to his knees.

He had travelled for hours on end
He was very sleepy as he just turned around a bend,
And over the cobbles he clattered and clanged
Then he found the old place called The Old Donkey Inn.
He went up to the landlord's daughter and then her father came and said,
'What are you doing here?'
And went to get his gun and shot the traveller dead!

Chloe Challinger (10)
Silverstone CE Junior School, Towcester

The Highway Puss

(Based on 'The Highwayman' by Alfred Noyes)

The light was a flashing bolt of lightning,
The corridor was a room tightening,
The cat flap was a monster laughing
And the cat came pouncing, pouncing, pouncing,
The cat came pouncing up to the bathroom door.

He had a sleek, black fur coat,
He had a white star on his throat,
He had a pair of boots,
He had a salute.

Over the carpet he pounced,
He tapped on the door with his finger,
To see a beautiful black-eyed cat
Pusie, the master's daughter,
Making a plat in the palm of her paw she sat.

In the hall another cat hissed,
Where Timmy the cat hissed,
His eyes were red, his nose rosy pink
And then Puss kissed her goodbye and headed for the haunted sink.

Hannah Sylvester (10)
Silverstone CE Junior School, Towcester

The Highway Baby

(Based on 'The Highwayman' by Alfred Noyes)

The wind was a stinging breeze,
The moon was a snow-white star,
The road was a smooth, gravely track
And the baby came crawling, crawling, crawling
The baby came crawling up to the haunted, spooky, candy pop castle.

He'd got a bald, shiny head,
A sticky dummy stuck to his nappy and a leather jacket that he wore,
He crawled up to the candy pop castle and knocked on the door
The door opened and out came the girl of his dreams, blue-eyed.

'I have a dry mouth, so off I go to get some milk and for you a
                                                    pink bow,'
So off he crawled to get some milk, crawling, crawling, crawling,
But while he was gone they sent a ton of baby agent men,

'Hello my sweet gorgeous, we're going to tie you up'
And there she screamed like a moaning pup.
The baby came back crawling, crawling, crawling,
The agents saw through the window,
They threw their dummies at the baby and he would not get back up,
So the baby went crawling, crawling, crawling no more.

Campbell Taylor (10)
Silverstone CE Junior School, Towcester

The Bad And Ugly

(Based on 'The Highwayman' by Alfred Noyes)

The wind was roaring like a mad lion,
The plane that Ugly Tommy was flying had icicles
And was now on fire, it was as hot as an iron,
He jumped out and launched his parachute,
Flying, flying, flying, ugly Tommy was flying like a bird.

Behind Ugly Tommy, came down a lovely red plane and then . . . *bang!*
It had blown up; smashing and damaged it fell on fire,
Ugly Tommy arrived back on the ground and car jacked a blue Toyota
Speeding, speeding, speeding, Tommy was speeding along to
Ammunition.
As soon as Ugly Tommy went into the shop the man died because he
was so ugly
Tommy took all of the guns and ammo and got back in the car to kill
his enemy!

Ugly Tommy went to the High Roller Casino to kill his enemy, the
gambler
He went in and put on shades,
He saw his enemy and hid behind the big baby statue, his enemy was
gambling
Ring-ring, ring-ring, Tommy's phone started to ring,
Ugly Tommy picked it up, it was his old friend, Small Smoke, he said,
'We need to go down to the big mansions'
So Tommy, being ugly and all went down to the big haunted mansion
He went in and there it was, the thing he needed, the sapphire ruby,
He got it and got out and then there were blue soldiers, the enemy,
and he died.

Jordan Knight (10)
Silverstone CE Junior School, Towcester

Kane

(Based on 'The Highwaymen' by Alfred Noyes)

The wind was a screaming dead person,
The moon was a silver, shiny, sapphire moon,
The road was a deserted school
And Kane came riding, riding, riding
Kane came riding up to the haunted zoo.

He had a red blood mask on his face
And drove a tank into the haunted zoo
And he had a blood-red suit.

Over the bars he crushed and bruised
He smashed the zoo shop with his fist, the cops were there
Kane managed to get out of jail
And got a double-barrelled shotgun.
In the lion cage he went,
Down to the circus
Off to Ant World and set free all the ants
Then he got arrested.

Nathan Rogers (10)
Silverstone CE Junior School, Towcester

The Ghost Bride

(Based on 'The Highwayman' by Alfred Noyes)

The wind was a haunting breeze,
The moon was a clear sight,
The road was a silent path,
And then the ghost bride came,
Flying, flying, flying
The Ghost Bride came flying up to the old church.

She'd got an old, ripped wedding dress on,
And she'd go around saying, *'Whoo'*
She had chains which would clatter and clang,
And that night when the church bell went *bang*,
Out came a man, a man, a man,
And out came a man who floated up to the old church.

She found him and loved him,
And found out his name was Tim,
He was dressed up in a torn suit,
That was held together with a pin, a pin, a pin,
That was held together with a pin.

Now there is no Ghost Bride
But a ghostly couple who float around,
Laughing, laughing, laughing
They float around laughing in the old church.

Isabel Garriock (10)
Silverstone CE Junior School, Towcester

The Highway Horse

(Based on 'The Highwayman' by Alfred Noyes)

The wind was a mixture of peace and hope,
The moon was a light of a star,
And the Highway Horse came trotting, trotting, trotting,
The Highway Horse came trotting up to the abandoned western town.

He had a pure brown coat with a mane of glistening silver,
His hooves clopped on the sandy floor, his tail swished in the faint smell of ale,
And his rider stepped into the tavern.
He had a gallop so swift it could be felt a mile away,
He was the Highway Horse.

The horse charged to the stable, one by one his hooves clattered on the rocky floor,
And who was waiting there?
But it was Miss Mable lying in the stable
He was able to see her side of beauty.

He let her sleep and crept away,
But something made him stay
He heard his rider scream
But it was too late; he had no time to escape
The men of King George shot him down, onto the gate and by his one true love.

Calum Kerns (10)
Silverstone CE Junior School, Towcester

The Highway Dog

(Based on 'The Highwayman' by Alfred Noyes)

The wind is a puff of smoke,
The moon a sphere of light,
The road a crashed up peanut
And the Highway Dog came howling, howling, howling,
The Highway Dog came howling up to the old dog shack.

The Highway Dog was well turned out,
And had a small based hat
He had a long, red coat
And posh boots on all four legs,
And his pistol glittered in the smoky, sky-light of the world.

The only thing that will beat the dog is one thing called love,
The Dalmatian beats his love,
For his heart is on hers,
So he jumped to the shack
And who should be there but his love, but dead!

The Highway Dog went mad,
He started to turn bad,
He ran towards the highway
And who should be there but King Dog's men,
And with a swift bang an old wreck of a car went past,
And King Dog's men ripped him apart,
And the Highway Dog went falling, falling, falling,
The Highway Dog went falling down to Hell!

Edward Measey (10)
Silverstone CE Junior School, Towcester

Untitled

I climbed the rat-infested stairway
Along the ghostly hall,
And gazed up at the portrait
Hanging on the wall.

The windows locked and bolted
Seemed alone to me,
They peered out at a lifeless view
Across the deserted lea.

My heart felt dead and rotten
My thoughts with anger ran wild,
Returning to that abandoned house
I first knew as a child.

Christina Cooper (11)
Silverstone CE Junior School, Towcester

Returning To That House

I climbed the shiny stairway
Along the sunny hall,
And gazed up at the picture
Hanging on the wall.

The windows gleamed and cracked
Seemed similar to me,
They looked out at a radiant view
Across the golden lea.

My heart felt content and joyful
My thoughts with excitement ran wild,
Returning to that blissful house
I first knew as a child.

Tiana Djahanbakhsh (11)
Silverstone CE Junior School, Towcester

The Haunted House

I climbed the ungainful stairway
Along the scareful hall,
And gazed at the pictures
Hanging on the wall.

The windows fastened and secured
Seemed foolish to me,
They watched out at a balmy view
Across the misty lea.

My heart felt dejected and heavy
My thoughts with fright ran wild,
Returning to that appalling house
I first knew as a child.

Oliver Hinton (11)
Silverstone CE Junior School, Towcester

Untitled

I climbed the sun-filled stairway
Along the crimson-bricked walls,
And gazed up at the ceiling bright
Standing on the wall.

The windows gleaming with content
Seemed cleaner than can be,
They over-shadowed a glorious view
Across the flowered lea.

My heart was filled with excitement
My thoughts with glee ran wild,
Returning to that fun-filled house
I first knew as a child.

Zuzanna Paveley (11)
Silverstone CE Junior School, Towcester

Untitled

I climbed the rasping staircase
Along the eerie hall,
And gazed up at the carcass
Hanging on the wall.

The windows, shattered and bashed
Seemed spine-chilling to me,
They look out at an appalling view
Across the forbidden lea.

My heart felt blood curdling
My thoughts with fear ran wild,
Returning to that hair-raising house
I first knew as a child.

Joe Read (11)
Silverstone CE Junior School, Towcester

Untitled

I climbed the rat-infested stairway
Along the ghostly hall,
And gazed up at the portrait
Hanging on the wall.

The windows locked and bolted
Seemed alone to me,
They peered out at a lifeless view
Across the deserted lea.

My heart felt dead and rotten
My thoughts with anger ran wild,
Returning to that abandoned house
I first knew as a child.

Aaron Culley (11)
Silverstone CE Junior School, Towcester

Untitled

I climbed the treacherous stairway
Along the eerie hall,
And gazed up at the silver sword
Hanging on the wall.

The windows, misty but dear
Seemed to be calling to me,
They bellowed out at a distant view
Across the long dead lea.

My heart felt cold and empty
My peculiar thoughts of death ran wild,
Returning to that loathsome house
I first knew as a child.

Emilie Sylvester (11)
Silverstone CE Junior School, Towcester

Memories

I climbed the peaceful staircase
Along the tranquil hall,
And gazed upon the joyful pictures
Hanging on the wall.

The windows so vibrant and stunning
Seemed to be smiling at me,
They gazed out at a dazzling view
Across the magnificent lea.

My heart felt warm and cheerful
My thoughts with glee ran wild,
Returning to that memorable house
I first knew as a child.

Anna Lawson (11)
Silverstone CE Junior School, Towcester

My Favourite Animal

His name was Bee
He was very special to me,
He was a dog
Who belonged to my uncle Rob.

He was quite hairy
But not too scary,
I cried when he died
But he will always be on my mind.

Francesca Hudson (8)
Silverstone CE Junior School, Towcester

My Rabbit

I have a black rabbit
He has got a funny habit
When he wants to eat more
He holds out a paw
When he sees food he just grabs it.

Adam Dearsley (7)
Silverstone CE Junior School, Towcester

Bloodcurdling House

I climbed the ghostly stairway
Along the spooky hall
And gazed up at the blood stain
Covering the wall.

The windows were spine-chilling and terrifying
Seemed to me they spied out across
The cool view
Across the grassy lea.

My heart felt like a bone
And my thoughts with blood ran wild
Returning to that bloodcurdling house
I first knew as a child.

Benjamin Webb (11)
Silverstone CE Junior School, Towcester

Untitled

I climbed the cheerful stairway
Along the outstanding hall
And gazed up at the angel
Hanging on the wall.

The windows new and gold
Seemed rich to me,
They faced out on an exciting view
Across the amazing lea.

My heart felt young and wild
My thoughts with happiness ran wild,
Returning to that full of life house
I first knew as a child.

Marcus Culley (11)
Silverstone CE Junior School, Towcester

The Rabbit Rap

His name is Willow
He has straw for a pillow
He lives in a hutch
And I love him very much.

He likes to drink water
Just like he oughta
He lives in a hutch
And I love him very much.

He likes to play in his run
He has a lot of fun,
He lives in a hutch
And I love him very much.

He likes to eat carrot
Because he's a rabbit not a parrot,
He lives in a hutch
And I love him very much.

His ears hang down
And he jumps like a clown,
He lives in a hutch
And I love him very much.

That's my Willow!

George Goodman (7)
Silverstone CE Junior School, Towcester

My Rabbit Flopsy

Flopsy is browny white
And very bright,
He loves to eat his lettuce
While I'm eating my breakfast,
He's very fluffy
And never scruffy.

I love him the most
He eats crispy toast,
Eating dandelions is what he likes most,
When I take him for a walk
I watch him like a hawk.

He loves to play throughout the day
With his bouncy ball that he pushes away,
He is a true friend
Till the very end.

Nicole Djahanbakhsh (8)
Silverstone CE Junior School, Towcester

Charlie Triever

I have a dog which is ginger
And he likes to hinder
His name is Charlie
He likes to chew his toy Barney
And he's a good active hound.

Sadly, he's a very old dog
But can be quite a hog
He loves his Bonio dog biscuits
I'd like to try it if I would risk it
And he's a good active hound.

He has a friend called Brewster
And he's as mischievous as a mouse
Every time he's home alone
He always wrecks the house
And he's a brutish little hound.

Charlie has turned out to be a good friend
But it might be coming to the end,
It's sad for him to be getting very old
Charlie is as precious to us as mighty gold
But still, he's a good active hound.

Maxwell Cawthorne (7)
Silverstone CE Junior School, Towcester

My Special Cat

I had a special cat called Lilly
She was very silly
She sat on the mat all day
And purred in a lovely way.

She liked to catch birds and mice
Which I thought was not very nice
She sat in the sun having some fun.

She liked to eat and lick her feet
She ran round the hall with her ball
She was brown and black with a spotted patch.

One day we thought she had gone to hide
We then found out that she had died
I miss my cat every day
I wish that she had stayed.

Hannah Pace (8)
Silverstone CE Junior School, Towcester

The Mist Makers

The mist makers, the mist makers
What fair hair
The mist makers, the mist makers
They're everywhere
The mist makers, the mist makers
Watch them glow
The mist makers, the mist makers
Look at them flow
The mist makers, the mist makers
Watch them go!
The mist makers, the mist makers
Kissing all the girls
The mist makers, the mist makers
Growing long curls
The mist makers, the mist makers
Pinching people's eyes
The mist makers, the mist makers
Got lovely thighs
The mist makers, the mist makers
I will never know.

Jake Van Kampen (9)
Silverstone CE Junior School, Towcester

Buster

I've got a little dog called Buster
He gets my mum all of a fluster
When he's playing with the feather duster
Always eating carrots or toast
But it's cheese he likes the most.

Christopher Hinton (8)
Silverstone CE Junior School, Towcester

Dog, Dog

Dog, dog, you're black and white
You can jump to a great height
You can even fly a kite
Dog, dog, you're alright.

Dog, dog, you sleep on my bed at night
When you're there, I don't get a fright
I won't let you out of my sight
Dog, dog, you're alright!

Thomas Elmstrom (7)
Silverstone CE Junior School, Towcester

Cats

He talks smartly
And his name is Parsley
He is not a girl
But he looks like a pearl
Shimmering in the dark.

Rue is sleek and fast
We know little about his past
He's a bit of a beast
And he likes to feast
On mice, rats and birds.

I have a cat, his name is Sully
He likes to chase and is a bully
He often sleeps upon my bed
He miaows and miaows until he's fed
His dinner of fresh fish.

Jack Haywood (8)
Silverstone CE Junior School, Towcester

My Four Hens

I've got four hens and they like to write with pens
They are very fluffy and quite fussy
They've got lots of fleas and like eating peas
They're orangey-brown and want to be crowned
They want to be queens and go on high beams
They like grass and would like to blow my brother's brass
They're really sweet and cuddly and sometimes quite ugly
These are my hens.

Emma Measey (8)
Silverstone CE Junior School, Towcester

The Mist Makers

The mist makers sigh
And they fill the sky
They are white and blurred
Like invisible fur
They live in the sea
And fill it with glee
But to passers-by
Well, they just sigh.
They cause havoc and confusion
Just like pollution
I am sorry to say
But they don't go away.

Madeleine Smee (9)
Silverstone CE Junior School, Towcester

The Mist Makers

The mist makers, the thoughtful and kind
Float across the twilight sky.
Their snowy fur, so long, so white
Can dazzle your eyes with just one look.
They love music, the mist makers do
And when they hear relaxing music they breathe a sigh of mist.
They protect the island with their foggy mist surrounding.

Shannon Webb (9)
Silverstone CE Junior School, Towcester

The Mist Makers

The mist makers are unique
They find what they find, seek what they seek.

They don't barge or push or pull or squish
They do not want to hurt or abolish.

These mist makers help this paradise
They do more than once, not twice, not thrice.

They do not have an ambition, none at all
They are shaped like pillows, never a ball.

The humans love the mist makers very much
Though they can't catch the mist makers, not even a clutch.

Christian Loveless (9)
Silverstone CE Junior School, Towcester

Mist Makers

Just as I saw one I had to run
Its shiny white coat was as big as a boat
Its big black feet were as big as a sheet
When I stopped running all was quiet . . . too quiet
I stepped forward, I heard a noise
I looked and I saw light so I walked up to it
It was a mist maker,
It was digging a hole.

Louis McKendry (9)
Silverstone CE Junior School, Towcester

The Mist Makers

The people love the mist makers.
They are gloomy white with brilliant hairs on their body.
But the only thing about them that is horrible, is the smell of the mist they make.
The mist smells of wet fur, wet, wet fur.
When it thunders the mist fades away into the distance.
Then when they are hungry they let out a terrible cry of hunger.
So they are the people's love of the island,
The wonderful mist makers.

Zoe Stockley (9)
Silverstone CE Junior School, Towcester

The Mist Makers

The mist makers, the guard of the people with their silky white fur.
All around them the sound of gentle sea washing against the shore.
The best thing about the mist makers is not the gentle sound of sea or
the silky fur,

But the foggy mist that comes out of their mouths,
That protects the people on the island.
But the only thing which makes the mist makers blow mist
Is the sound of gentle music.

Charlotte Lloyd (9)
Silverstone CE Junior School, Towcester

Mist Makers

They're white, what are they?
They float, how do they?
They live on an unknown island, where is it?
They're mist makers.

What do they do?
They make mist.

They're not just nice, they are important
We play music calm and soothing
They make the mist
Mist to hide us and to keep them safe.

Conor Young (9)
Silverstone CE Junior School, Towcester

The Mist Makers

Calm and soft, making whale sounds
Nice to the ears, mist makers, they swim through the air
Changing colours purple and green
Mist makers.

Jack Hales (9)
Silverstone CE Junior School, Towcester

Moon

Moony, Moony
Your eyes shine so bright
They remind me of moonlight
You are so cute
And your ears are minute
And I love you.

Your fur is so soft
And I love you lots and lots
Your paws are so clever
And I will love you forever
Curled up in your nest
To me you are the best.

Robyn Edwards (8)
Silverstone CE Junior School, Towcester

The Mist Makers

The mist makers, the mist makers are seeing their friend Clare
The mist makers, the mist makers don't know what to wear.
The mist makers, the mist makers are flying through the air.
The mist makers, the mist makers want to eat a pear.
The mist makers, the mist makers are dirtying the floor.
The mist makers, the mist makers are getting really bored.
The mist makers, the mist makers are shutting the door.
The mist makers, the mist makers are very poor.
The mist makers, the mist makers are running to town.
The mist makers, the mist makers are going far down.
The mist makers, the mist makers are truly an adventurous pair.

Emily Libich (9)
Silverstone CE Junior School, Towcester

Mist Makers

The people desire the mist makers
Because of their snow-white fur and glistening black eyes.
Some people like them because there's not one girl.
Some people like them because of their habitat.
But everyone loves them because of their soft marshmallow hearts.
They tremble with fear in case any humans come near.

Jonathan Howse (9)
Silverstone CE Junior School, Towcester

Untitled

I climbed the wrecked stairway
Along the dark hall
And gazed up at the lifeless man
Hanging on the wall.
The windows hideous and gloomy
Seemed scary to me
They connected out to a huge view
Across the foggy lea.
My heart felt dark and cold
My thoughts with fear ran wild
Returning to the bleak house
I first knew as a child.

Luke Heavey (10)
Silverstone CE Junior School, Towcester

Whee Poem

Whee goes the firework shooting in the sky
Whee scream the children.
Whee!
Whee goes the child on the roller coaster, zooming in the sky
Whee scream the children in the playground.
Whee!
Whee scream the alien flying his saucer.
Whee scream the children.
Whee!
Whee cry the children flying down the slide.
Whee scream the children in the playground.
Whee!
Whee scream the parents as the horse comes cantering through.
Whee scream the children,
Whee!

Leanne Wilson (9)
Swaffham Prior CE Primary School, Swaffham Prior

Bang

Bang!
A hammer when it hits a man's thumb.
Bang, bang!
When a door closes very fast,
When something is dropped from a high point.
Bang, bang, bang!
When a window is shut really hard.
Bang, bang!
When something hard hits the roof of a car.
Bang, bang!
When someone is hitting a table and
When something bursts,
It's bang, bang, *bang!*

Charlotte Elston (9)
Swaffham Prior CE Primary School, Swaffham Prior

Vroom

A car on a race track
Vroom!
A bus on the road
Vroom, vroom!
The air brakes on a bus.
Vroom!
A plane on a runway
Vroom!
A motorcycle zooming off.

Richard Terrington (8)
Swaffham Prior CE Primary School, Swaffham Prior

Rustle

The rustle of feet walking through autumn leaves.
Rustle, rustle!
The sound of a tiger prowling through the grass.
Rustle, rustle!
The rustle of trees blowing in the wind.
Rustle, rustle!
The sound of plastic bags being rubbed together.
Rustle, rustle!
The rustle of a flag blowing in the wind.
Rustle, rustle!
The sound of ice cracking and a man falling through.
Rustle, rustle!
The rustle of a person turning the pages in a book.
Rustle, rustle!
The sound of paper being rolled up into a ball.
Rustle, rustle!
The sound of a pencil being sharpened.
Rustle, rustle!
The sound of a hedgehog going through a bush.
Rustle, rustle!

Hannah Eaton (9)
Swaffham Prior CE Primary School, Swaffham Prior

The Cherry Muncher

Can anybody tell me please
I really want to know
What has two legs like hoses
And picks its noses?

Or what has fur
Is it a he or a her?
It has feet like half-eaten cherries
It doesn't look very merry.

And tell me please
Does it like biting knees?
It's got purple and blue wings.

Oh what is it?
It looks like a bird,
It has a helicopter head
It's jumping on my bed.

Emilia Hubbard (7)
Swaffham Prior CE Primary School, Swaffham Prior

Yep

Can anyone tell me please,
I definitely want to know, what has two belly buttons
And a frog's head on its toes, in a red satin skirt?
Oh what has fire eyes
And toes all over his ears
And a snake on his head
And it loves Mummy dear?

And tell me what
Has whiskers on its legs
And lighting for arms
And a nose made of slime
And it drinks beers?

What has a combed hair?
Tell me quick, it's eating my ear!

Harry Doe (9)
Swaffham Prior CE Primary School, Swaffham Prior

Slam!

Slam!
An alien's tentacle whacking a human's head,
Slam!
An anvil falling on a man's foot,
Slam!
An alien spaceship knocking down a building,
Slam!
A man being whacked on the head by an old lady's umbrella.
Slam!

Adam Tarasewicz (8)
Swaffham Prior CE Primary School, Swaffham Prior

Can Anybody Tell Me?

Can anybody tell me please
About the ugly thing
Who's covered in scratchy fleas
And says ring-a-ding-ding?

Oh what has rings on its nose
And prickles on his ears?
Oh what has flippers on its toes
Has he got any fears?

And tell me about its mouth
Does it breathe fire?
Why does he live in the south?
Deep in Swaffham Prior?

Oh what is the creature
Who's in my room?
Wherever he is,
I'll whack him with a broom!

Henry Kingsmill (9)
Swaffham Prior CE Primary School, Swaffham Prior

Blood-Red Eyes

Can anybody tell me please
Tell me what is barking outside my window
With blood-red eyes?
Sometimes I get so scared
I run to my parents' bed.

Oh what has it got? Dragon ears
And a devil's tail
The spike is on fire,
Also he has a scaly back,
As hard as steel lines on his head.

And tell me has it had dinner?
Because I hate scary things
Oh what is upstairs
Past my parents' room,
In my bathroom?
It's opened my door
It has pulled my covers off
Got in, pulled the covers up
And pushed me out of bed
And now it's asleep in my bed!

Emma Hodge (8)
Swaffham Prior CE Primary School, Swaffham Prior

Whee

Whee went a man rolling down the hill, *whee*.
Whee went the car when it was sliding.
Whee went the mouse freshly caught in the mousetrap.
Whee went the moth being blown by the wind.
Whee went the water boat when it fell down the water hill.
Whee went the man on the motorcycle.
Whee went the man that ran out of petrol.
Whee went the lorry making a turn.
Whee shouted the people on the roller coaster.
Whee what?
Whee how!

Kasia Tabecka (8)
Swaffham Prior CE Primary School, Swaffham Prior

Smash!

A man smashing the window
Smash, smash.
A dragon flying down into a frozen lake.
Smash.
Glass falling onto a massive stone.
Smash, smash, smash!

Smash.
A stone smashing ice.
Smash.
The sound of glass and a stone bashing together.
Smash, smash, *smash!*

Rosie Robinson (8)
Swaffham Prior CE Primary School, Swaffham Prior

Fizz

The lemonade bottle as you open the lid.
Fizz.
It fizzes on your tongue as you put it in your mouth.
Fizz, fizz, fizz.
You sit and watch TV and popcorn fizzes in your mouth.
Fizz.
The motorbike fizzes as your dad turns it on.
Fizz, fizz, fizz.
What a lot of fizz noises.

Maddie Lewinski (8)
Swaffham Prior CE Primary School, Swaffham Prior

Slam

Slam, oh no I dropped a bit of glass.
Slam, slam, slam.
My mum hit my brother with a hammer.
Slam, my grandma put her eyes back in,
Slam, slam, slam, slam, slam
Slam, slam, slam, slam, slam!
That is a word you will never forget.

Jessica Hill (8)
Swaffham Prior CE Primary School, Swaffham Prior

Rustle

A hedgehog rustling in the leaves.
Rustle, rustle.
A dog looking for rats in the hay.
Rustle, rustle, rustle.
A hamster on his wheel.
Rustle what?
A horse galloping across the field.
Rustle, rustle.
A horse itching his hind leg with his teeth.
Rustle, rustle, rustle.
A polar bear walking through the snow.
Rustle.
A horse jumping a hurdle.
Rustle.
A mouse running in the hay.
Rustle, rustle.
A horse rustling in the straw.
Rustle, rustle, rustle.

Cleo McGregor (8)
Swaffham Prior CE Primary School, Swaffham Prior

Roar!

The distant roar of motorbikes as they fly into action.
Roar, roar, roar!
Roar, roar, roar!
The roar of my mum when she is angry.
Roar!
The roar of motorbikes as they zoom into action.
The roar of a lion who is trying to scare hyenas.
The roar of an angry tiger chasing his enemy.
Roar!
The distant roar of motorbikes as they fly into action.
Roar, roar, roar!
Roar, roar, roar!
The roar of my mum when she is angry.
Roar!
The aeroplane engine roars as it comes to life.
Roar!
The roar of the angry lion which can be heard many miles away.
Roar!

Ayshea Blanks (8)
Swaffham Prior CE Primary School, Swaffham Prior

Fizz

When I went to the pub I opened up a can of Coke and it was all fizzing.
Fizz, fizz, fizz!
It fizzes in your mouth as you put a mint in your mouth.
Fizz, fizz!
You sit and watch TV and popcorn fizzes in your mouth.
Fizz, fizz!
The fizz of the popcorn as it pops, pops, pops in the machine.
Fizz, fizz!
The fizz of the sun as it sizzles and lets out light.
Fizz, fizz!
The eardrum fizzing as it pops.
Fizz, fizz!
The fizz of the lemonade bottle as you open the lid.
Fizz, fizz!
It makes a fizzy noise when you turn on the engine.
Fizz, fizz!

Becky Arksey (8)
Swaffham Prior CE Primary School, Swaffham Prior

Squeak

Squeak, squeak.
A toddler pretending to be a mouse, *squeak, squeak.*
A car that desperately needs oil, *squeak, squeak.*
Squeak, squeak what?
Two squeaks of guinea pigs cuddling together.
Squeak, squeak.
Which guinea pigs?
The squeak of the pushchair with the babies in it.
Squeak?
The squeak of the wind going through the trees.
Squeak of a rat that's going to be killed.
Squeak, squeak, squeak, *squeak!*

Mia Blanks (8)
Swaffham Prior CE Primary School, Swaffham Prior

Help

Can anybody tell me please
I really need to know
What has spiky knees
And one green scary toe?

Oh what has hair like a wild bush
And feet like tiger paws?
What has a strong and scary push
And ten black pointed claws?

And tell me, tell me, tell me now
What it likes to eat?
It looks like it could eat a cow
An enormous amount of meat.

Oh what is that howling sound downstairs?
Making me so scared
It's different colours with lots of hair
My favourite ribbon got flared.

Helena Pumfrey (8)
Swaffham Prior CE Primary School, Swaffham Prior

Boom

Someone is jumping into a pool, why? Where?
Someone is shooting in mid-air!
A car crashing, better not be my car,
There's a thing outside and it goes,
Boom, boom, boom, boom!
It's Bigfoot!

Jake Atkin (9)
Swaffham Prior CE Primary School, Swaffham Prior

Zoom!

A car goes zoom as it goes past.
Zoom, zoom!
The fireworks zoom straight in the sky.
Zoom!
A rocket zooms to outer space.
A race track makes the sound of zooming off.
Zoom, zoom, zoom!
A shooting star zooming along the stars.
Zoom!

Qia McKenna (9)
Swaffham Prior CE Primary School, Swaffham Prior

Crunch

The crunch of a peanut being squashed by a train.
Crunch.
The munching and crunching of someone eating.
Crunch, crunch.
Walking on warm pebbles at the beach.
Crunch.
Paper being crunched and crammed into a ball.
Crunch, crunch.
Crunch of me biting into a nice juicy apple.
Crunch.
Rustling, crunching paper bags together.
Crunch, crunch.
A person gobbling a cashew nut.
Crunch.
Someone walking down a gravel path.
Crunch.
Crunch!

Emma Luton (8)
Swaffham Prior CE Primary School, Swaffham Prior

The Hacker

Can anybody tell me please
About the thing
That has eyes in its mouth
And flabby bits upon its chin?

Oh what has a tail that always points south
Is nothing but a sin
Six or seven more arms
And carries a chainsaw?

And tell me what has claws on its palms
And just wants more
Runs on four legs and black claws?

Oh what is smiling wickedly?
Oh someone call the police
Firemen or ambulance
Please, please someone please help
It's hacking down my house!

Matthew Hobbs (9)
Swaffham Prior CE Primary School, Swaffham Prior

Splash!

Splash!
A dragon falling into a bowl of custard.
Splash!
Splash, splash!
A man jumping into the sea.
Someone filling up a paddling pool, splash!
Splash!
Splash?
A stone being dropped into a pond.
A girl washing her face, *splash! Splash!*
Splash! Splash! Splash!

Lily Armstrong (9)
Swaffham Prior CE Primary School, Swaffham Prior

Help

Can anybody tell me please
What has four eyes and seventy-one knots in his hair, please?
What has skin purple, brown, pink and green
I wonder, and has three noses and one mouth, I cannot tell.
And tell me, what has a dragon tail?
Oh please, oh please, oh please, tell me now this minute.
Oh what is playing on my bike and with my toys?
Please, oh please!
It's in my bedroom asleep, in my bed, oh please get it out this second.

Reece Jones (8)
Swaffham Prior CE Primary School, Swaffham Prior

SATs

Why do we have tests?
I need some rest
Cry, cry, cry
Why, why, why?
Just get up and revise
Just go on Revise Wise.
I had a terrible morning
I woke up yawning,
Run, run, run,
So much fun,
School is bad,
Science is sad,
SATs are over
No more worries,
Go to lots of trips,
Have a lot of fun,
Zoom, zoom, zoom!
Zoom into your room.

Maria Akhtar (11)
The Beeches Primary School, Peterborough

The Worst Week Of My Life

SATs are here
I'm still full of fear
I felt like a nervous wreck
Because my hands were shaking, as fast as a drill
I thought it was going to be an easy course
But when the time came it was
Except for the science of course.

When the time came I felt excited
I started jumping everywhere
I was annoying my parents there
The night before I revised, revised and revised even more
During the actual SATs I felt they were easier then I thought
Even easier than mocks.

When the SATs were ending
I started bending
I was the happiest person on Earth
SATs had ended,
But then I thought that mocks were never worthwhile
I am worried about my results
They might be good, they might be bad
You never know!

Tamina Amjad (11)
The Beeches Primary School, Peterborough

Poem About SATs

I am nervous,
I am scared
I want to cheat
But I am still prepared.

It is hard and difficult
I cannot think because
My brain has fallen out.

Finally, they are over
I am happy as a king
But I am still scared for my results
Hooray, hooray! SATs are over. Hooray, hooray! SATs are over!

Usmaan Tanveer (11)
The Beeches Primary School, Peterborough

Walking To School

My friends are fools
They always tease me at school
They play cricket but they always lose.

Then one day they gave me good news
I was in the cricket team and I couldn't refuse
I wanted to play when I started school.

After a while I thought they weren't fools
So that's why we are cool
When playing cricket at school.

Shoaib Iblal Aziz (11)
The Beeches Primary School, Peterborough

The Unforgettable Week

SATs, SATs, SATs,
Before SATs I felt as happy as a snake
Or as happy as a chef baking a cake
In a lake.
SATs, SATs, SATs,
Before SATs, I felt as pleasant as I could ever be
Until I was warned by Mr Lee-Smith
To open my brain with the magic key.
SATs, SATs, SATs,
What should I do?
I was as white as a canoe
Gazing in the sky that was clear blue.
SATs, SATs, SATs,
During SATs, I was mad,
I was sad,
I was now a maniac.
SATs, SATs, SATs,
I felt as bright as the sun
Now every day's fun.
SATs, SATs, SATs,
My results are unpredictable,
They also are unreliable,
SATs are over, it's indescribable!

Madeeha Aurangzeb (11)
The Beeches Primary School, Peterborough

The Week That Time Forgot

The week before the SATs went OK
I splashed on cream to vanish my red face, called Olay.
I revised like a madman
Most of the electricity went on the fan
Because my brain needed to refresh
I was so stupid I could eat human flesh.

When the SATs were here
I woke up deaf from my left ear
So I couldn't hear what people were saying
I felt so terrified
My friends were horrified
But I worked my way through them
And when they were over
I was happier than Noah.

After the SATs had gone
I was allowed to do anything I want
My brother felt like an ant
My mum shouted to him, 'You can't!'
While I was feeling smirky
My brother was murky
And I felt good
And I knew I should.

Umar Shafiq (11)
The Beeches Primary School, Peterborough

The Week That I Will Never Forget

I'm nervous, I'm worried
What should I do?
Yeah revise, revise, revise!
Come on Sareena, hurry
You need some describing words
You might describe a creature
For goodness sake Mr Lee-Smith
It's easy for you because you're a teacher.

Are the answers right?
What if they're wrong!
Oh God, please help me
Look, there's a question of something bright.

They were easy
I could do them in two seconds
Maths was hard
Science was peasy
I was happy
I was a bit curious
I was worried
What will my results be?

Sareena Kauser (11)
The Beeches Primary School, Peterborough

The Week That Had No End

My parents said, 'Revise, revise and revise'
Should I or should I not?
I thought I'd done the lot
I didn't have any cares in the world, but
When I came to school I was all bare
'Revise, revise, revise,' said Mr Lee-Smith but it was OK for him as well,
he was free.

The week was disturbed by tests
It was like a tongue-twister never to be said
I couldn't find my mind, I thought it was coded
Tick-tock, tick-tock, the hands on the clock were 9.30
I went to bed early
But my brain turned out all curly wurly.
Boom, boom, boom, boom went my broken heart
Cluck, cluck, cluck went my nerves
It was too late, the papers were collected in
'Right,' went Mr Lee-Smith, distracting my nervous breakdown
I couldn't believe it, it was incredible
Maths, English and science all were finished
Fun begins now!

Hamreena Younas (11)
The Beeches Primary School, Peterborough

The Week That Would Never End

One, two, I've got the flu
Three, four, I'm such a bore
Five, six, I'm eating Weetabix
Seven, eight, I'll play with my mate
Nine, ten, oh no! SATs are here again.

It's as hard as juggling
But I'm not struggling
I'm really worried about my test
Don't worry, I'll do my best
Science is easy
Maths is hard
English is peasy, I give my sister a card
What will be my test marks?
I'll have to go and see.

I'm free at last because I look like a bumblebee
Now it's boring
All I can hear is my dad snoring
I'm free as sand
I can make my own band
Now I can play cricket
My job is to stand behind the wicket.

Kanwal Hussain (11)
The Beeches Primary School, Peterborough